Peterson Field Guides®
For Young Naturalists

Caterpillars

Jonathan P. Latimer

Karen Stray Nolting

Illustrations by Amy Bartlett Wright

Foreword by Virginia Marie Peterson

Houghton Mifflin Company
Boston 2000

FOREWORD

My husband, Roger Tory Peterson, traced his interest in nature back to an encounter he had with an exhausted flicker when he was only 11 years old. When he found what he thought was a dead bird in a bundle of brown feathers, he touched it and the bird suddenly exploded into life, showing its golden feathers. Roger said it was "like resurrection." That experience was "the crucial moment" that started Roger on a lifelong journey with nature. He combined his passion for nature with his talent as an artist to create a series of field guides and paintings that changed the way people experience the natural world. Roger often spoke of an even larger goal, however. He believed that an understanding of the natural world would lead people — especially young people — to a recognition of "the interconnectedness of things all over the world." The Peterson Field Guides for Young Naturalists are a continuation of Roger's interest in educating and inspiring young people to see that "life itself is important — not just ourselves, but all life."

— **Virginia Marie Peterson**

The authors would like to thank Paul A. Opler, who reviewed and critiqued the manuscript, for his invaluable suggestions. Thanks also to Paul E. Nolting for his continued support and encouragement.

Latimer, Jonathan P.
Caterpillars / Jonathan P. Latimer, Karen Stray Nolting ; illustrations by Amy Bartlett Wright ; foreword by Virginia Marie Peterson. p. cm.
Summary: Describes the physical characteristics, behavior, and habitat of a variety of caterpillars, arranged by the categories "Smooth," "Bumpy," "Sluglike," "Horned," "Hairy," "Bristly," and "Spiny."
ISBN 0-395-97942-0. — ISBN 0-395-97945-5 (pbk.)
1. Caterpillars Juvenile literature. [1. Caterpillars.] I. Nolting, Karen Stray. II. Title.
QL544.2.L38   2000   595.78'139—dc21   99-38944   CIP

Book design by Lisa Diercks. Typeset in Mrs Eaves and Base 9 from Emigre.
Manufactured in the United States of America
WOZ 10 9 8 7 6 5 4 3 2 1

CONTENTS

DISCOVERING CATERPILLARS

Bumpy . . . Spiny . . . Hairy . . . Bristly. . . . These words might make you think of something scary, but they are also used to describe a fascinating little creature—the caterpillar. Caterpillars are one amazing stage in the life cycle of a group of insects we know as butterflies and moths.

This book will help you understand and identify some of the caterpillars (also called larvae) you are likely to see where you live. It uses the method of identification invented by the man who revolutionized field guides, Roger Tory Peterson. He created a simple system of drawings and pointers (now known as the "Peterson System") that call attention to the unique marks on each kind of caterpillar. It can help you answer the question *What kind of caterpillar is that?*

What Kind of Caterpillar Is That?

At first glance, all caterpillars may look very much alike to you. A closer check will reveal big differences between caterpillars. Here are some questions you can ask when trying to identify a caterpillar.

What Does the Caterpillar Look Like? Caterpillars are slow-moving and make tempting targets for birds and other predators. But some have developed horns or spines that help them avoid being eaten. Others rely on camouflage and concealment to escape. Because of this, the appearance of a caterpillar's body is one of the easiest ways to distinguish one caterpillar from another. That is why the caterpillars in this book are arranged according to the way their bodies look. When you want to identify a caterpillar, start by matching it to one of the following categories.

Smooth—These caterpillars are hairless. They are smooth from one end to the 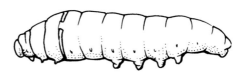 other, although they may be fatter in the middle.

Bumpy—Some caterpillars have bumps or knobs on their bodies. These bumps often have hairs sticking out of them.

Sluglike—Fatter and shorter than most other caterpillars, some of these are hairless while others are covered with fine hairs or down.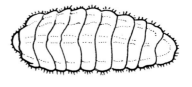

Horned—Some caterpillars have developed horns that are used for defense. Others have thick, fleshy threads called 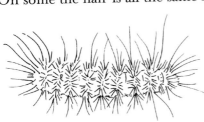 *filaments* on their bodies.

Hairy—Hairy caterpillars are covered with a coat of hair. On some the hair is all the same length. Others have some longer hairs mixed with short ones. Sometimes the longer hairs stick out in clusters or tufts.

Bristly—The bodies
of some cater-
pillars look like
small scrub
brushes. They are
covered with short,
stiff hairs that stick out in all directions.

Spiny—The most threatening-looking caterpillars have
sharp spines on their bodies. These spines often have

 branches with
sharp
points.

What Color Is the Caterpillar? Color is another clue
to the identity of a caterpillar. As with an adult butterfly, a
caterpillar's color can serve several different roles. Some
caterpillars are green or black, which helps them blend
with the color of leaves or twigs. Others are brightly colored, which warns predators that the caterpillar is bad-
tasting or even poisonous. The color pattern of some
caterpillars resembles bird droppings, which makes birds
totally ignore them.

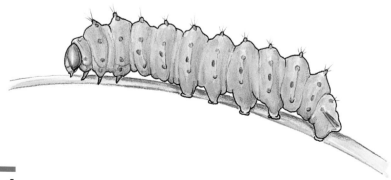

What Plant Is the Caterpillar on? Most caterpillars spend their entire life on one plant, which is known as a *host plant*. The female moth or butterfly lays its eggs on the host plant. When the eggs hatch, the caterpillars start eating.

When you look for caterpillars, look all around the plant. They may hide on the underside of leaves or conceal themselves in the litter at the bottom of a plant. A few even burrow into the ground. You may have to look carefully to find them.

Don't Touch

Most caterpillars can't hurt you, but a few can irritate your skin if they are handled. Others, such as the Io Moth caterpillar, have spines that protect them from predators. They can give you a painful sting.

Looking at a Caterpillar It is sometimes hard to tell which end of a caterpillar is which. At first glance, a caterpillar looks like a worm that has 13 segments. But a caterpillar is an insect. It has three parts like other insects—the head, the thorax, and the abdomen.

The Head—A caterpillar's head is often small and can sometimes be pulled into its body for protection. The head contains the caterpillar's eyes and mouth. Caterpillars have poor eyesight, but they can distinguish colors and shapes. They use their eyes to find the right plant for feeding. Like

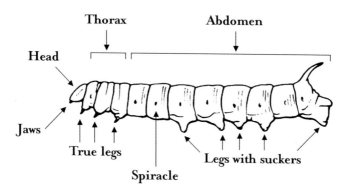

Thorax Abdomen Head Jaws True legs Spiracle Legs with suckers

most insects, caterpillars have jaws, called *mandibles,* to chew leaves.

The Thorax—A caterpillar has three pairs of legs near its head. Those legs will become the three pairs of legs on the adult butterfly or moth. Each leg ends with a small claw that is used to grasp things, such as the edge of a leaf. The three segments these legs are attached to make up the thorax of the caterpillar.

The Abdomen—The remaining ten segments of a caterpillar are its abdomen. It has five legs that look like suckers. They anchor a caterpillar to a leaf or a twig and keep it from falling off.

If you look closely at a caterpillar, you may notice small holes in the sides of some segments. These are called *spiracles.* A caterpillar breathes by drawing air into its body through these holes.

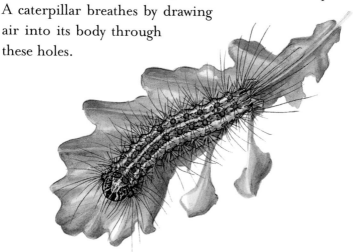

The Life Cycle of Butterflies and Moths One of the most remarkable things about butterflies and moths is their life cycle—the stages they pass through during their lives. Caterpillars are really the second stage of that cycle. The first stage is the egg.

Egg—A caterpillar's life begins when an adult female lays her eggs. Most butterflies and moths lay their eggs on the leaves or stems of a plant that will serve as food for the caterpillar. A few lay theirs in the litter beneath the plant.

The majority of female butterflies or moths lay 100 or more eggs during their lifetime, but some may lay as many as 6,000! Many lay their eggs one at a time, but others, such as Gypsy Moths, lay them in clusters of 100 or more.

Most eggs are about the size of the head of a pin. They are dull-colored to help conceal them from bugs or beetles that might eat them. Some eggs contain food for the

developing caterpillar, others contain poisons that help prevent them from being destroyed by predators. Some eggs hatch a few days after they are laid.

Caterpillar—This is the stage when a butterfly or moth does almost all of its growing. When a caterpillar comes out of its egg, it is a tiny creature, less than half an inch long. Its role is to grow as quickly as possible to its full size, so a caterpillar starts eating as soon as it hatches. Some caterpillars eat more than 25,000 times their body weight before they reach full-size!

In order to grow, a caterpillar must shed its skin. This usually happens four times during the caterpillar stage. Once a caterpillar is fully grown, it stops eating and begins looking for a place to go through its next stage. The caterpillar's skin then splits one last time, revealing the pupa. Many moth caterpillars use their silk to spin a cocoon that surrounds the pupa.

Silk

Most caterpillars produce slender strands we know as silk. These strands harden in the air into a tough fiber. Caterpillars use silk in many ways. Tent Caterpillars use silk to build large nests that house many individuals. They feed together near the nest at night and rest inside during the day. Other caterpillars, such as the Painted Lady, dine alone. They build a nest at the tip of a branch and eat the leaves inside. Some, such as the Silver-spotted Skipper, use silk to tie two leaves together or to curl a leaf into a tube that is used as a nest. Many moth caterpillars spin *cocoons*. The cocoon protects the pupa as the caterpillar changes into an adult moth.

Pupa—This is the stage when the caterpillar turns into an adult butterfly or moth. The pupa has a hard shell. It cannot crawl around or fly. Most pupae are brown, reddish, or green to help them blend into the background. Some look like leaves. A butterfly pupa is called a *chrysalis*.

Many moth caterpillars burrow into the ground under a rock or in leaf litter and rest there. Others create cocoons to protect their pupae. Hairy species often mix their hairs with silk to make a cocoon.

Inside the hard shell of the pupa, a butterfly or moth is forming. After several weeks or even months, the butterfly or moth emerges.

Adult Butterfly or Moth—The adult that comes out of the pupa looks nothing like the caterpillar that it came from. The primary goal of a butterfly or moth is to find a mate and lay eggs, which starts the cycle all over.

Keeping Track

Many people keep a list of all the caterpillars they have ever seen. This is called a "Life List." You can begin yours with the list on page 48. It includes all the caterpillars described in this book.

GIANT SWALLOWTAIL

A young Giant Swallowtail caterpillar looks so much like a bird dropping that it is able to escape some predators! Birds simply ignore it. If a bird does disturb the caterpillar, it uses another defense. Two red-orange horns pop out from behind its head and release a foul odor.

The Giant Swallowtail caterpillar is sometimes called an Orange Dog or Orange Puppy in the South. It feeds on the leaves and young shoots of citrus trees and is often considered a pest. Citrus growers sometimes spray their groves with insecticide to eliminate this caterpillar.

Giant Swallowtails spend winter as a chrysalis, and adults emerge in spring. Female Giant Swallowtail butterflies produce 500 or more eggs, laying them one at a time near the tips of leaves or twigs.

Did You Know?
- With a wingspan of 6 inches, the Giant Swallowtail butterfly is one of the largest in North America.
- Giant Swallowtail butterflies beat their wings slowly, but they fly fast because of their large size. When they are drinking nectar, they often flutter their wings.

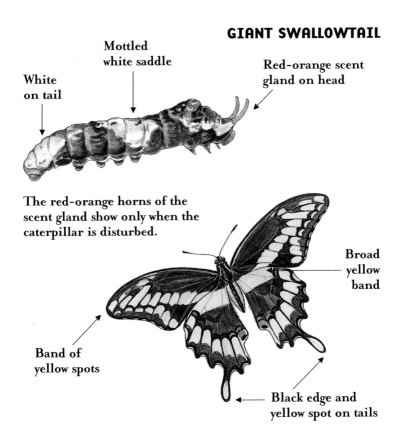

White
on tail

Mottled
white saddle

Red-orange scent
gland on head

The red-orange horns of the
scent gland show only when the
caterpillar is disturbed.

Broad
yellow
band

Band of
yellow spots

Black edge and
yellow spot on tails

Favorite Plants Giant Swallowtail caterpillars are
found on trees and plants of the Citrus family, especially
orange and tangerine. Adult butterflies sip nectar from
many plants, including lantana, azalea, bougainvillea, and
swamp milkweed.

When To See Them Giant Swallowtails can be seen
from May to August in the North and throughout the
year in Florida and the Deep South, southern Texas,
southern California, and Arizona.

Habitat Giant Swallowtails are found in many places,
including hillsides near streams or gullies, pine forests,
towns, and citrus groves.

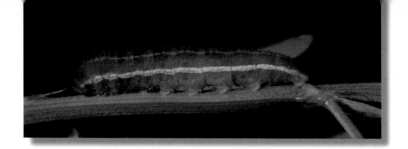

CLOUDED SULPHUR
and ORANGE SULPHUR

The bright green caterpillars of Clouded Sulphurs and Orange Sulphurs look so much alike that even experts have trouble telling them apart. They feed mostly at night. Both caterpillars eat clover and alfalfa, but the main food of Orange Sulphurs is alfalfa, which is why they are sometimes called Alfalfa Butterflies. As more farmers have planted these crops, Clouded Sulphurs and Orange Sulphurs have spread across North America. Their caterpillars are sometimes considered pests.

Clouded Sulphur butterflies are often found in meadows or clover and alfalfa fields with their close relatives, Orange Sulphur butterflies. Both look very much alike, but there is a difference—most Orange Sulphurs have orange in their wings, while Clouded Sulphurs do not. Some females of both species are white.

Did You Know?
• Young sulphur caterpillars chew holes in the tops of leaves, then eat the leaf from the tip down. Older caterpillars eat one half of a leaf first, then the other half.
• Clouded Sulphurs and Orange Sulphurs hibernate through winter as caterpillars.
• The Clouded Sulphur is sometimes called the Common Sulphur.

CLOUDED SULPHUR and ORANGE SULPHUR

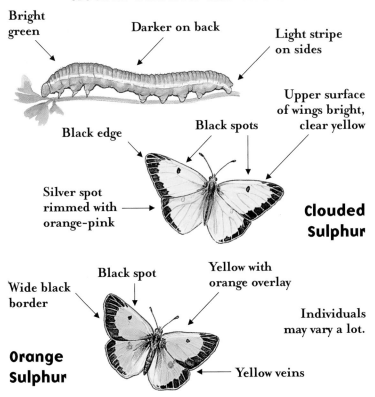

Bright green

Darker on back

Light stripe on sides

Upper surface of wings bright, clear yellow

Black edge

Black spots

Silver spot rimmed with orange-pink

Clouded Sulphur

Black spot

Yellow with orange overlay

Wide black border

Individuals may vary a lot.

Orange Sulphur

Yellow veins

Favorite Plants Caterpillars of Clouded Sulphurs and Orange Sulphurs can be found on alfalfa and clover. Adults sip nectar from many kinds of flowers, including dandelions, milkweeds, goldenrods, and asters.

When To See Them Clouded Sulphur caterpillars and Orange Sulphur caterpillars can be seen all year in the South and during winter where they hibernate.

Habitat Clouded Sulphurs and Orange Sulphurs are found throughout most of the United States and southern Canada. They can be seen in a wide variety of open areas, including alfalfa and clover fields, lawns, road edges, and meadows.

COMMON WOOD-NYMPH

Common Wood-Nymph caterpillars hatch from their eggs in fall. Unlike most caterpillars, they do not immediately start eating. Instead, they look for a place to hibernate until spring. As the weather warms, they begin feeding. Their only food is grass, and they feed mostly at night. During the day they hide in the grass. Their color and pattern help conceal them from predators.

Common Wood-Nymph butterflies have distinctive eyespots on their wings, which gives them one of their common names—Goggle Eye. Eyespots are a special form of defense against predators. When a Common Wood-Nymph butterfly is startled, it spreads its wings and displays its eyespots. This often distracts a predator or even scares it away.

Did You Know?

• Male Common Wood-Nymph butterflies patrol grassy areas with an irregular, jumpy flight, looking for females. Females are less active and often rest in the shade. Their brown color blends into the color of tree bark.

• The markings on Common Wood-Nymph butterflies can vary greatly in different locations. Because of this, it has been given dozens of common names, including Large Wood-Nymph, the Goggle Eye, and the Blue-eyed Grayling.

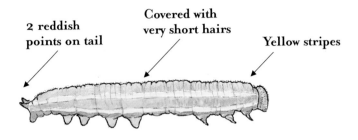

2 reddish points on tail

Covered with very short hairs

Yellow stripes

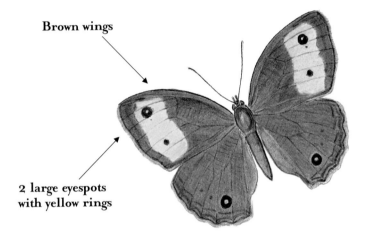

Brown wings

2 large eyespots with yellow rings

Favorite Plants Common Wood-Nymph caterpillars can be found on grasses. Adults feed very little, but they sometimes sip juice from rotten fruit or flower nectar.

When To See Them Common Wood-Nymph butterflies can be seen from late May to October. Caterpillars can be seen throughout fall, winter, and early spring.

Habitat Common Wood-Nymphs can be found throughout southern Canada and most of the United States. They can be seen in sunny, grassy areas including prairies, open meadows, marshes, and fields.

SILVER-SPOTTED SKIPPER

You can recognize a Silver-spotted Skipper caterpillar by the unusual way it protects itself during the day. In the morning it cuts a circular flap in a leaf. Then it folds the flap over itself and secures it with silk. This shelters the caterpillar and conceals it from predators while it rests until nightfall, when it begins to munch on leaves. As the caterpillar grows, it builds larger shelters. Eventually, it spends the day resting between two leaves loosely held together with silk.

Adult skippers share qualities with both butterflies and moths. They have thick bodies and are usually brown or black like many moths. However, skippers are active during the day like butterflies.

Did You Know?
• Skippers get their name from their swift, powerful flight, which looks like a stone skipping across water. They are usually faster than other butterflies but fly shorter distances.

SILVER-SPOTTED SKIPPER

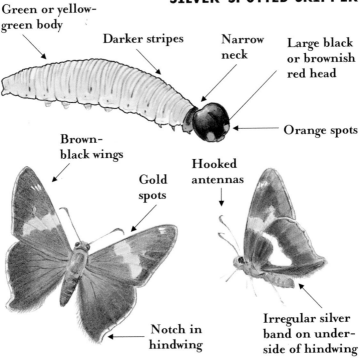

Green or yellow-green body

Darker stripes

Narrow neck

Large black or brownish red head

Orange spots

Brown-black wings

Gold spots

Hooked antennas

Notch in hindwing

Irregular silver band on underside of hindwing

Favorite Plants Silver-spotted Skipper caterpillars are found on locust trees or wisteria. Adults drink nectar from common milkweed, red clover, and thistles. They also sip at mud puddles.

When To See Them Silver-spotted Skipper caterpillars can be found during spring in the North and the West. In most of the East they can be found during spring and summer. Adult butterflies can be seen from May to September in most of the North and West and from February to December in the Deep South.

Habitat Silver-spotted Skipper caterpillars can be found on their food trees. Butterflies can be seen in open woods and meadows or in suburban areas from southern Canada to northern Mexico.

VICEROY, RED-SPOTTED PURPLE, and WHITE ADMIRAL

Although these three butterflies have very different markings, their caterpillars look very much alike. The young caterpillars hang a ball made out of bits of leaves and silk off the leaf they are eating. The ball swings in the wind and it may distract predators. In fall the caterpillars build a shelter out of leaves, securing it to a twig with silk. They spend winter inside this shelter.

Viceroy and Red-spotted Purple butterflies not only taste bad to predators, they also mimic, or imitate, other bad-tasting butterflies. Viceroys look like Monarch butterflies, and Red-spotted Purples resemble Pipevine Swallowtails. These bad-tasting butterflies have bold colors that warn predators to beware. Once a predator has tasted one of these butterflies, it is unlikely to go after anything that looks like it.

Did You Know?
- These caterpillars look like bird droppings, which may fool predators.
- Red-spotted Purples and White Admirals are considered the same species.
- The Viceroy butterfly is the official state insect of Kansas and Kentucky.

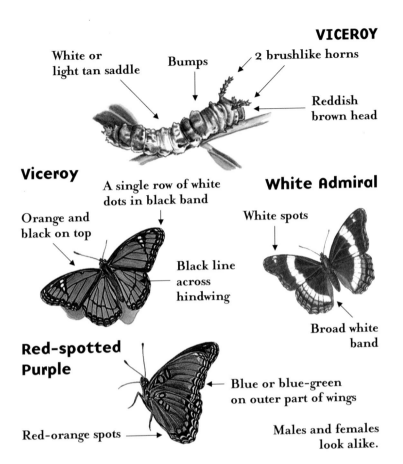

VICEROY

White or light tan saddle

Bumps

2 brushlike horns

Reddish brown head

Viceroy

A single row of white dots in black band

Orange and black on top

Black line across hindwing

White Admiral

White spots

Broad white band

Red-spotted Purple

Blue or blue-green on outer part of wings

Red-orange spots

Males and females look alike.

Favorite Plants All three of these caterpillars can be found on willows and poplars. Viceroys can also be seen on cottonwoods. Red-spotted Purples also eat wild cherry and aspens. White Admirals can be found on birches.

When To See Them Viceroys can be seen from May to September. Red-spotted Purples and White Admirals can be found from April to October.

Habitat Viceroys are found in damp, marshy areas and along streams. Red-spotted Purples are found in drier wooded areas. White Admirals are usually found in cooler, more northern areas.

POLYPHEMUS MOTH

In Greek mythology, Polyphemus was a Cyclops—a giant with one eye located in the center of his forehead. The spots on this giant moth's lower wings reminded people of this character and gave the moth its name.

Adult Polyphemus Moths emerge from their cocoons in late afternoon and mate that night. The following evening the female lays her eggs. The caterpillars hatch after about 10 days and begin eating leaves. Polyphemus Moths do all their eating in the caterpillar stage. The adult moth cannot eat or drink.

Polyphemus caterpillars reach their full growth—almost 4 inches long—after about 50 days. In August or September they spin a cocoon, often with a leaf bound to its surface. They spend winter in the cocoon and emerge as adults in spring.

Did You Know?
- Polyphemus caterpillars feed alone.
- Older caterpillars eat an entire leaf and then cut its stem at the base so that it falls to the ground. This may help conceal signs of their feeding from predators.
- When disturbed, the Polyphemus Moth quickly beats its wings, flashing its eyespots. This may scare off some predators.

POLYPHEMUS MOTH

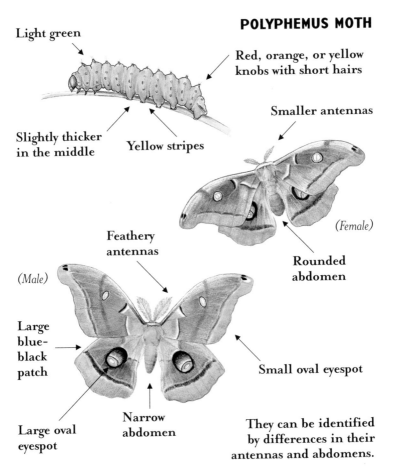

Light green

Red, orange, or yellow knobs with short hairs

Slightly thicker in the middle

Yellow stripes

Smaller antennas

(Female)

Feathery antennas

Rounded abdomen

(Male)

Large blue-black patch

Small oval eyespot

Large oval eyespot

Narrow abdomen

They can be identified by differences in their antennas and abdomens.

Favorite Plants Polyphemus caterpillars feed on a wide variety of trees and shrubs, including oak, willow, maple, and birch. They also can be found on apple, beech, ash, grape, and pine. Adults do not feed.

When To See Them Polyphemus moths can be seen throughout summer. They are often attracted to lights at night.

Habitat Polyphemus Moths are found in forests, urban areas, orchards, and wetlands. They can be seen through-out most of southern Canada and the United States.

GRAY HAIRSTREAK

G ray Hairstreak caterpillars can vary in color from green to yellow to red-brown. The diagonal stripes on their sides can range from white to reddish purple. No matter what color they are, these caterpillars look a lot like slugs.

Gray Hairstreaks produce 2 or more generations each spring and summer. The last generation hibernates through winter as a pupa, and adults emerge in spring and lay eggs. Gray Hairstreak caterpillars sometimes damage bean, corn, or cotton crops. In some places they are known as Cotton Square Borers because young caterpillars bore holes in cotton plants to feed. Hairstreak butterflies get their name from their short threadlike tails. The Gray Hairstreak is the most widespread hairstreak in North America.

Did You Know?

- A Gray Hairstreak caterpillar can pull its head into its body when it is surprised.
- Gray Hairstreak butterflies fly fast and close to the ground.
- The caterpillars of other hairstreaks look very similar to the Gray Hairstreak.

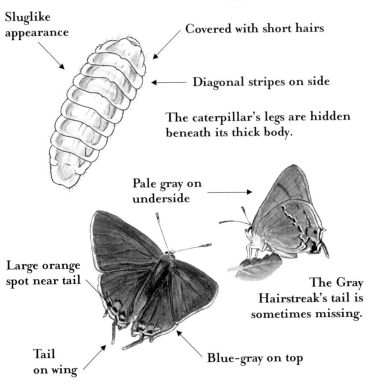

Sluglike appearance

Covered with short hairs

Diagonal stripes on side

The caterpillar's legs are hidden beneath its thick body.

Pale gray on underside

Large orange spot near tail

The Gray Hairstreak's tail is sometimes missing.

Tail on wing

Blue-gray on top

Favorite Plants Gray Hairstreak caterpillars can be found on the flowers and fruits of an almost endless variety of plants, including beans, clovers, cotton, mallows, and snapdragons. Adults sip nectar from many flowering plants, including milkweeds, mints, goldenrods, and white sweet clover.

When To See Them Gray Hairstreaks can be seen from May to September in the North and from February to November in the South.

Habitat Gray Hairstreak caterpillars can be found on their food plants, often in farmers' fields. They range throughout the United States from southern Canada to Mexico.

SPRING AZURE

Spring Azures are one of a few caterpillars that seem to have made a sweet deal with ants. They "bribe" the ants to look after them during the day when they are resting by producing honeydew, a sweet liquid that ants use for food. In return, the ants protect the caterpillar from predators such as beetles and wasps. At night the Spring Azure caterpillars feed on flowers. Other caterpillars, including some hairstreaks and blues, are also protected by ants.

Spring Azures hibernate through winter as a chrysalis. Dark blue Spring Azure butterflies emerge almost as soon as the weather begins to warm in spring.

Did You Know?

• Spring Azure caterpillars feed mainly on flowers. Their choice depends on what flowers are in bloom when they hatch.

• Spring Azures are often the first butterfly you will see in spring. Later in the year they are joined by Summer Azures, which look very similar.

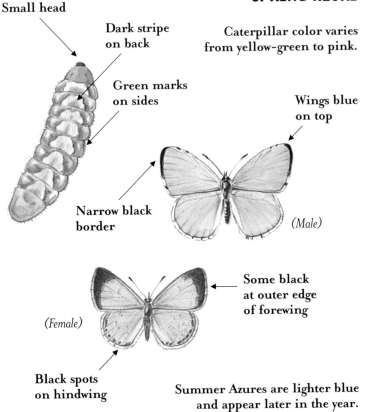

Small head

Dark stripe
on back

Caterpillar color varies
from yellow-green to pink.

Green marks
on sides

Wings blue
on top

Narrow black
border

(Male)

Some black
at outer edge
of forewing

(Female)

Black spots
on hindwing

Summer Azures are lighter blue
and appear later in the year.

Favorite Plants Caterpillars eat flowers from a variety
of shrubs and trees, especially those with clusters of flowers,
such as dogwood, viburnum, and cherry. Adults sip nectar from dogwood, blackberry, and many others.

When To See Them Spring Azures can be found from
January to May along the Gulf Coast and from May to
July in Canada.

Habitat Spring Azures can be found in clearings, along
the edges of woods, and in freshwater marshes and
swamps. They range as far north as Alaska and Canada
and throughout most of the United States.

HORNWORMS

Hornworms are serious pests for gardeners and farmers. They chew their way through the leaves and young fruit of tomatoes, potatoes, and other plants, leaving great holes and spoiled fruit. They eat during the day as well as at night.

The adult moth emerges in May or June. It lays its eggs on the underside of the leaves of tomato, tobacco, or other plants. The eggs hatch after about a week, and the eating begins. When the hornworms are fully grown, they burrow 3 to 4 inches under the soil. There they shed their skin and become a pupa.

Did You Know?
- The horns of these hornworms cannot hurt people.
- It takes 28 to 36 days for a hornworm to reach full-size. They eat almost constantly during that time.

An important natural enemy of hornworms is a small wasp that attaches its cocoon to the hornworm's body. When the wasp emerges, it destroys the hornworm. Often several wasps will attach themselves to a single hornworm.

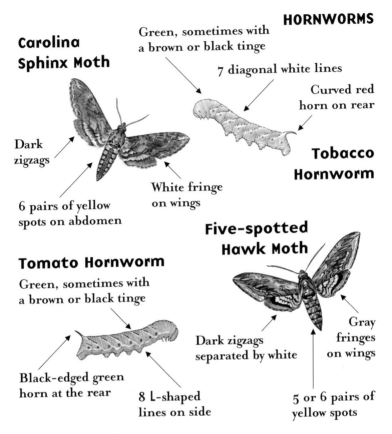

HORNWORMS

Carolina Sphinx Moth

Green, sometimes with a brown or black tinge

7 diagonal white lines

Curved red horn on rear

Dark zigzags

Tobacco Hornworm

White fringe on wings

6 pairs of yellow spots on abdomen

Five-spotted Hawk Moth

Tomato Hornworm

Green, sometimes with a brown or black tinge

Dark zigzags separated by white

Gray fringes on wings

Black-edged green horn at the rear

8 L-shaped lines on side

5 or 6 pairs of yellow spots

Hornworms are large, sometimes more than 4 inches long.

Favorite Plants Both these hornworms eat the leaves and fruit of tobacco, tomato, eggplant, pepper, potato, and some weeds.

When To See Them The Carolina Sphinx Moth and the Five-spotted Hawk Moth can be seen flying at dusk over flowers such as petunias in May and June. The hornworms appear throughout summer.

Habitat You can find hornworms in almost any garden or field that contains the proper food plants. They are pests in many places.

29

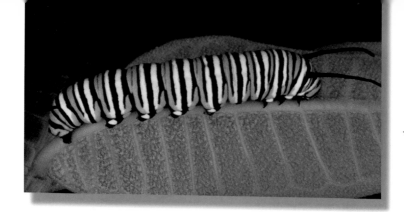

MONARCH

Monarch caterpillars only eat one thing: the leaves of milkweed plants. Milkweeds are named for the thick milky juice in their leaves and stems. This juice has chemicals in it that taste bad to most animals, but not to Monarchs. As a Monarch caterpillar eats a milkweed leaf, these chemicals collect in its body, passing the bad taste to the caterpillar and eventually to the adult butterfly. Adult Monarchs are easy to spot, but birds quickly learn not to eat them because they taste bad. The Monarch's bright colors warn birds not to attack them.

Monarch butterflies migrate south each fall to escape the bad weather of winter. Female Monarch butterflies lay eggs as they return north in spring. Monarch caterpillars can be seen from spring to fall.

Did You Know?

• It takes about a month for a Monarch to grow from an egg to an adult butterfly.

• Female Monarch butterflies deposit a single egg on a milkweed leaf or bud and then fly on. The egg hatches into a caterpillar, and it begins eating.

• The Monarch is the state butterfly of Alabama, Illinois, and Vermont.

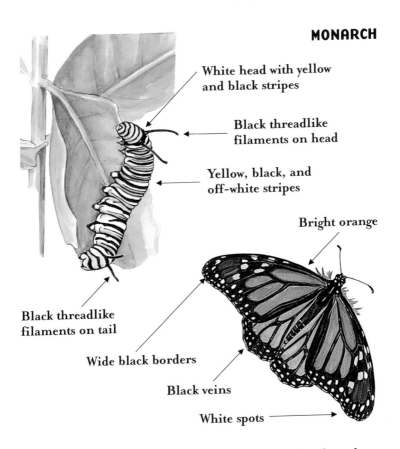

White head with yellow and black stripes

Black threadlike filaments on head

Yellow, black, and off-white stripes

Bright orange

Black threadlike filaments on tail

Wide black borders

Black veins

White spots

Favorite Plants Monarch caterpillars can be found on the underside of the leaves of most kinds of milk-weeds, especially in late summer or fall. Adult Monarchs sip nectar from all milkweeds but also visit other flowers.

When To See Them Monarchs can be found throughout North America from spring to fall. They may be seen all year in Florida, southern Texas, and southeastern California.

Habitat Monarchs can be found in almost any open area, including fields, meadows, weedy areas, marshes, and roadsides. They range from southern Canada throughout all of the United States, except Alaska.

PIPEVINE SWALLOWTAIL

The caterpillar of the Pipevine Swallowtail looks more like a monster than a caterpillar. It has hornlike filaments on every part of its body and two small red spots on its stomach that give out a foul odor. Fortunately, it is only about 3 inches long!

You may find many Pipevine Swallowtail caterpillars together, especially on a pipevine, the plant that gives them their name. They eat all parts of the plant, including leaves and stems. Like the Monarch caterpillar, they absorb chemicals from the pipevine, which makes them taste bad to birds and other predators. Adult Pipevine Swallowtails also taste bad, and five other butterflies mimic their markings, including the Red-spotted Purple (pages 20-21).

Did You Know?

- When a Pipevine Swallowtail caterpillar moves, it swings its head back and forth, making its filament wiggle. This may protect it from parasites or predators.
- When a full-grown caterpillar finds a place for its pupa, it anchors its hind feet with silk and spins a thread around its back like a seatbelt. This arrangement holds the pupa in place after it has shed its skin for the last time.

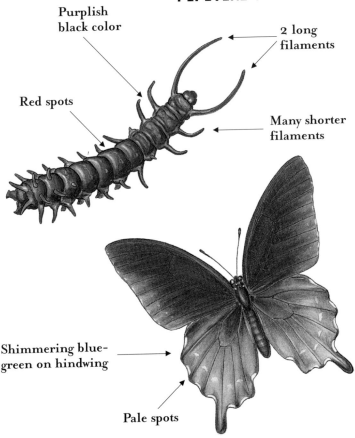

Purplish black color

2 long filaments

Red spots

Many shorter filaments

Shimmering blue-green on hindwing

Pale spots

Favorite Plants You can find Pipevine Swallowtail caterpillars on various pipevines. Butterflies sip nectar from honeysuckle, swamp milkweed, lilac, azalea, and thistle.

When To See Them In the Deep South you can see Pipevine Swallowtails from February to November. Farther north they can be seen from April to September.

Habitat Pipevine Swallowtails can be found in open glades in woods. In the West they are also found in open fields and scrub land.

GYPSY MOTH

A native of Europe and Asia, the Gypsy Moth was introduced into Massachusetts in 1868 or 1869 by Leopold Trouvelot. He brought Gypsy Moth eggs from Europe and planned to raise them for their silk. His experiment was a failure, and some of the moths escaped. Since then, they have slowly spread across eastern North America. Today, Gypsy Moth caterpillars are considered a pest. They strip the leaves off millions of trees every year.

Gypsy Moth caterpillars travel in a very unusual way, known as "ballooning." Newly hatched caterpillars climb to the tops of trees and dangle on threads of silk. The wind then carries them to nearby trees. Gypsy Moths also travel when people accidentally carry eggs or caterpillars to new locations.

Did You Know?

- During large infestations, you can hear the sound of Gypsy Moth caterpillars nibbling on leaves.
- Gypsy Moths survive winter as eggs. Eggs laid in July do not hatch until the following April or May.
- Adult female European Gypsy Moths cannot fly, which limits how fast the species can expand its range. Adult female Asian Gypsy Moths do fly, and their species may spread much faster if it becomes established.

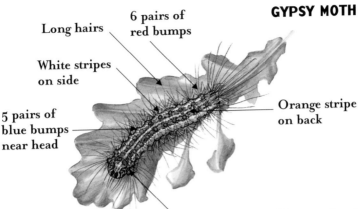

6 pairs of
red bumps

Long hairs

White stripes
on side

5 pairs of
blue bumps
near head

Orange stripe
on back

Black and yellow markings on head

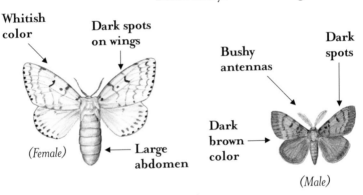

Whitish
color

Dark spots
on wings

Dark
spots

Bushy
antennas

Dark
brown
color

(Female) Large
abdomen

(Male)

Adult females are larger than males.

Favorite Plants Gypsy Moth caterpillars eat the leaves
of more than 300 different kinds of trees and shrubs,
but especially oaks. Adult Gypsy Moths do not feed.

When To See Them Gypsy Moth caterpillars begin
hatching in April and May. By the end of June the caterpillar stage is usually completed, and they spin cocoons. It
takes about two weeks to change into an adult moth.

Habitat Gypsy Moths can be found in forests and on
trees almost anywhere. They range from the northeastern
United States and eastern Canada to parts of the Southeast
and Midwest. Their range is slowly but steadily expanding.

35

TENT CATERPILLARS

You will probably see this caterpillar's silky white tent before you find the actual caterpillar. Tent caterpillars hatch from their eggs early in spring. A group of caterpillars immediately begins spinning their tents on the tips of branches just as new leaves are appearing. Tent caterpillars feed outside of their tent but return to rest during the day.

Tent caterpillars shed their skins four times during their five- to six-week growing period. When they are about 2 inches long, they abandon the tent. You may see hundreds of them crossing sidewalks and streets or crawling on buildings. Soon they find a sheltered place to spin their cocoon. About two weeks later adult moths emerge. They mate the first day and begin laying eggs. The eggs last through winter and hatch in spring.

Did You Know?
• Tent caterpillars lay down a trail of fine silk from their tent to the place where they feed. These trails are used as maps by other tent caterpillars.
• The California Tent Caterpillar is also known as the Western Tent Caterpillar.

TENT CATERPILLARS

Eastern Tent Caterpillar

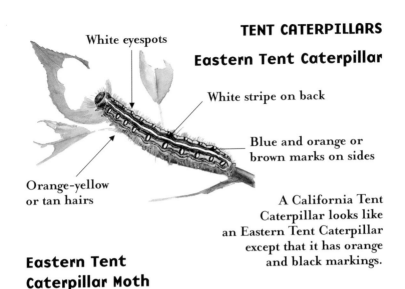

White eyespots

White stripe on back

Blue and orange or brown marks on sides

Orange-yellow or tan hairs

A California Tent Caterpillar looks like an Eastern Tent Caterpillar except that it has orange and black markings.

Eastern Tent Caterpillar Moth

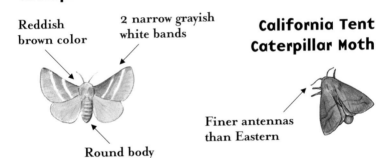

Reddish brown color

2 narrow grayish white bands

Round body

California Tent Caterpillar Moth

Finer antennas than Eastern

Favorite Plants Tent caterpillars feed on leaves. Their tents can be found in wild cherry and other fruit trees such as apple, crabapple, peach, and plum, and many other trees.

When To See Them Eastern Tent Caterpillars can be seen throughout the United States and southern Canada east of the Rocky Mountains. California Caterpillars can be seen in most of the West.

Habitat Tent moths can be found on their food plants in forests, orchards, and gardens. Large outbreaks of tent caterpillars can severely damage trees.

WOOLLY BEAR CATERPILLARS

Woolly Bears get their name from their short bristly hairs. There are several caterpillars called Woolly Bears. Each turns into a different moth. The caterpillar of the Isabella Tiger Moth is the Woolly Bear seen most often in the East and Midwest. The width of the reddish brown band around its middle is said to predict how cold or mild the next winter will be, but these predictions are not very accurate.

The Salt Marsh Caterpillar is solid yellow or orange. It is sometimes called the Yellow Woolly Bear. Its adult form is the Acrea Moth, which is found throughout the United States.

Did You Know?
- Woolly Bears roll up when they are disturbed.
- Woolly Bears curl up in fallen leaves and hibernate during winter. In spring a Woolly Bear spins a cocoon made out of its woolly hair. It uses its silk to hold the hairs together. The adult moth emerges several weeks later.
- Like the spines of a porcupine, the hairs on a Woolly Bear protect it from predators. Except for cuckoos, few birds eat Woolly Bears.

WOOLLY BEAR CATERPILLARS

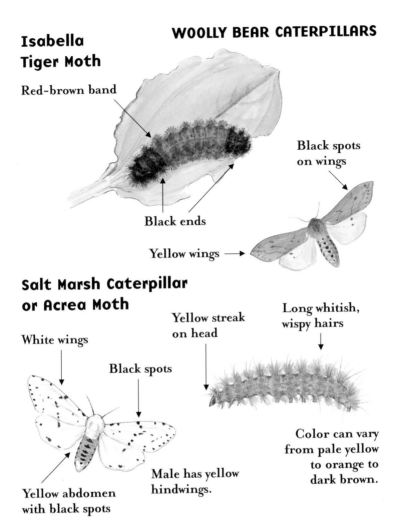

Isabella Tiger Moth

Red-brown band

Black ends

Yellow wings →

Black spots on wings

Salt Marsh Caterpillar or Acrea Moth

White wings

Black spots

Yellow abdomen with black spots

Male has yellow hindwings.

Yellow streak on head

Long whitish, wispy hairs

Color can vary from pale yellow to orange to dark brown.

Favorite Plants The Woolly Bear caterpillars of Isabella Tiger Moths feed on dandelion and many other low grasses or weeds. Salt Marsh Caterpillars feed on many weeds.

When To See Them Fall is the best time to see Woolly Bears. That is when they crawl about, looking for a place to hibernate.

Habitat Woolly Bears can be seen wherever their food plants are found, but especially in woods and marshes.

RED ADMIRAL

Red Admiral caterpillars come in so many colors that they may be difficult to identify. Young caterpillars eat and live within a shelter made from folded leaves. Older caterpillars make a nest by tying leaves together with silk. They are usually found on nettle plants.

Sometimes you can get very close to a Red Admiral butterfly without disturbing it. Some will fly out to investigate you, and they might even land on you. You may see the same butterfly in the same place several days or even weeks later.

Did You Know?
• The flight of a Red Admiral butterfly is rapid and very erratic.
• Red Admiral butterflies often perch in sunny places. They spread their wings to take in the sun's warmth.

Red Admirals cannot survive where it freezes in winter. They migrate north each spring from the South. By summer they can be found in most of North America. Where the weather is milder, Red Admiral butterflies sometimes hibernate through winter.

Narrow white stripes

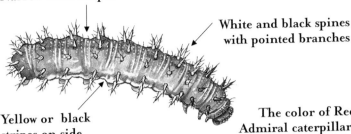

White and black spines
with pointed branches

Yellow or black
stripes on side

The color of Red
Admiral caterpillars
ranges from black to
yellow-green.

Black on top

White spots

Red-orange band
on forewing

Red-orange
band on edge
of hindwing

The Red Admirals you see in summer
are larger and brighter colored than
the ones you see in winter.

Favorite Plants Red Admiral caterpillars eat the leaves
of plants in the Nettle family. Red Admiral butterflies sip
sap from trees and juice from rotting fruit.

When To See Them Red Admirals can be seen from
March to October in most of North America. From
October to March they can be found in south Texas and
Mexico.

Habitat Red Admirals can be found in woods, yards,
parks, marshes, and wet fields. During migration they can
be found in almost any habitat. They range from Central
America and Mexico throughout the United States to
northern Canada and southern Alaska.

PAINTED LADY

Painted Lady caterpillars can be found most often on thistle plants. A caterpillar builds a webbed nest out of silk and leaves near the top of the plant. It stays inside its nest and feeds on the thistle. The nest protects it from predators and the weather. Painted Lady caterpillars also build nests on asters, daisies, hollyhocks, everlastings, mallows, and many other plants.

In warm areas, Painted Lady butterflies can survive through winter, but cold weather kills off the Painted Ladies in the North. Every few years, large numbers of Painted Lady butterflies fly from the deserts of northern Mexico and recolonize the continent in spring. Next to the Monarch, this is the most amazing migration by a butterfly in North America.

Did You Know?
- The Painted Lady caterpillar is found on thistle so often that it is sometimes called the Thistle Butterfly.
- The Painted Lady is the most widespread butterfly in the world. Because of this, it is also called the Cosmopolitan.
- Painted Lady butterflies fly straight and fast, but they sometimes dance erratically in the air.

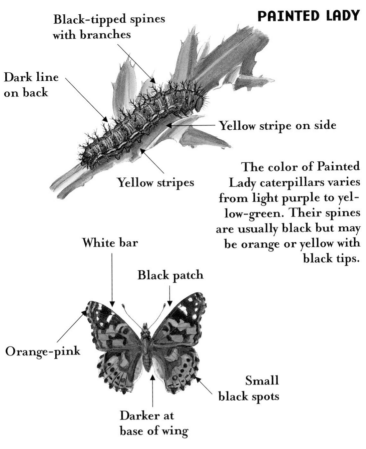

Black-tipped spines with branches

Dark line on back

Yellow stripe on side

Yellow stripes

The color of Painted Lady caterpillars varies from light purple to yellow-green. Their spines are usually black but may be orange or yellow with black tips.

White bar

Black patch

Orange-pink

Small black spots

Darker at base of wing

Favorite Plants Painted Lady caterpillars have been found on more than 100 different plants but most often on thistles, hollyhock, and mallow. Adults prefer nectar from thistles, aster, and ironweed.

When To See Them Painted Ladies can be seen from May to October and may be found during winter in the Southwest and southern California.

Habitat Painted Ladies can be found in open areas almost anywhere, including gardens. They migrate from the deserts of northern Mexico throughout the United States and Canada south of the Arctic.

COMMON BUCKEYE

Common Buckeye caterpillars live alone. The female lays a single egg on a leaf bud or on the top of a plant leaf and then moves on to lay her next egg some distance away. When the eggs hatch, the caterpillars begin eating. They often feed on the leaves of snapdragons or acanthus. They also eat plants that many gardeners consider weeds. Because of this, Common Buckeye caterpillars are sometimes put in gardens to control unwelcome plants.

You may find male Common Buckeye butterflies perched on low plants or bare ground during the day watching for females. They fly out occasionally to patrol or to chase other flying insects. Their zigzag flight can be very fast.

Did You Know?
- The eyespots on Common Buckeye butterflies may be used to scare away predators.
- Both Common Buckeye caterpillars and adults can survive through winter but only where it doesn't freeze. In fall many Common Buckeyes migrate and spend winter in the South.

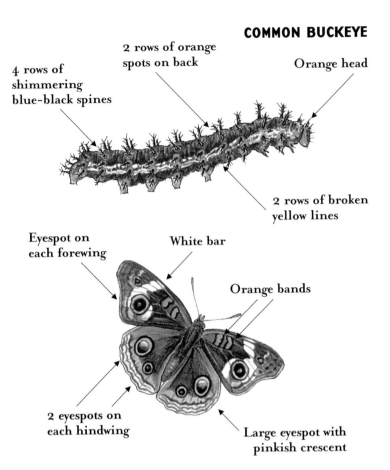

2 rows of orange spots on back

4 rows of shimmering blue-black spines

Orange head

2 rows of broken yellow lines

Eyespot on each forewing

White bar

Orange bands

2 eyespots on each hindwing

Large eyespot with pinkish crescent

Favorite Plants Common Buckeye caterpillars can often be found on snapdragons, plantains, or acanthus. Common Buckeye butterflies sip nectar from asters, chicory, knapweed, and sunflowers.

When To See Them Common Buckeyes can be seen from May to October in the North and throughout the year in the South.

Habitat Common Buckeye butterflies are found in open, sunny areas with low vegetation and some bare ground such as fields, dirt roads, streambeds, or dunes.

IO MOTH

Young Io Moth caterpillars feed together in a group. Sometimes they follow each other as they search for food, forming long lines that look like trains. As they grow older, Io Moth caterpillars move apart and feed alone. Io Moth caterpillars also change color as they grow older. Newly hatched caterpillars are orange, and their bristly spines are gray. Older caterpillars have green bodies with a red and white stripe on each side. Their branched spines are green with black tips.

When an Io Moth caterpillar reaches full-size, it spins a papery cocoon in the litter beneath its host plant or in a crevice in its bark. The adult Io Moth emerges during late morning or early afternoon and searches for a mate into the late evening.

Did You Know?
- Warning: The spines of an Io Moth caterpillar can give a painful sting if they are touched, so be careful if you handle them.
- If an Io Moth caterpillar is disturbed, it will often curl up and fall to the ground to get away.

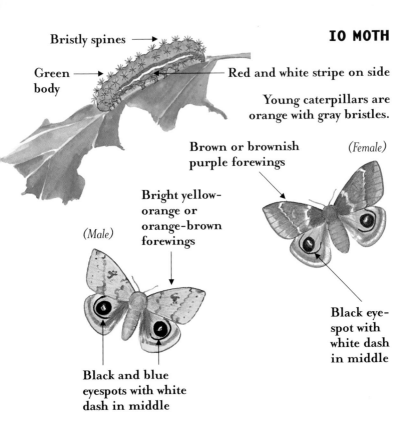

Bristly spines →

Green → body

Red and white stripe on side

Young caterpillars are orange with gray bristles.

Brown or brownish purple forewings

(Female)

Bright yellow-orange or orange-brown forewings

(Male)

Black eye-spot with white dash in middle

Black and blue eyespots with white dash in middle

Favorite Plants Io Moth caterpillars feed on many kinds of trees, including birches, elms, maples, oak, and willows. They can also be found on corn, roses, clover, currant, and blackberry plants. Adult moths do not feed.

When To See Them Io Moth caterpillars appear in spring or early summer and can occasionally be found in fall. In the Florida Keys they can be found all year.

Habitat Io Moth caterpillars can be seen in deciduous forests, thorn scrub, and suburban areas from the Atlantic Coast of the United States and southern Canada to the Dakotas, Nebraska, Colorado, Texas, and New Mexico. They are also found as far south as Costa Rica.